THE RISE, FALL & DEMISE OF AMY WINEHOUSE

(A MEMOIR)

WRITTEN BY: AMANDA GERALDINE

TABLE OF CONTENTS

PREFACE

Amy Jade Winehouse was an English singer and songwriter who was renowned for her wide range of musical styles, which included soul, jazz, and rhythm and blues, as well as her rich, expressive contralto voice.

Winehouse, who was a young member of the National Youth Jazz Orchestra, joined Simon Fuller's 19 Management in 2002. She quickly began recording songs before agreeing to a publishing deal with EMI. Through these record labels, she also established a professional working relationship with producer Salaam Remi.

Frank, Winehouse's self-titled debut album, was released in 2003. Apart from two covers, most of the album's songs had jazz influences and were co-written by Winehouse. In the UK, Frank received favorable reviews and was shortlisted for the Mercury Prize. Her song "Stronger Than Me" earned her the Ivor Novello Award from the British Academy of Songwriters, Composers, and Authors for Best Contemporary Song.

Back to Black, Winehouse's follow-up album was released in 2006 and went on to become one of the best-selling records in UK history as well as an international hit. She won the British Female Solo Artist award at the 2007 Brit Awards, where she was nominated for British Album of the Year. She received a second Ivor Novello Award for the song "Rehab." She became the first British woman to win five Grammys at the 50th Grammy Awards in 2008, tying the previous record for the most wins by a female artist in a single night. Her five awards included three of the General Field "Big Four" Grammy Awards: Best New Artist, Record of the Year, Song of the Year (for "Rehab"), and Best Pop Vocal Album.

Winehouse battled addiction and substance abuse. At the age of 27, she passed away on July 23, 2011, from alcohol poisoning. Back to Black momentarily overtook her as the best-selling record of the twenty-first century in the UK after her passing. On their list of the 100 Greatest Women in Music, VH1 rated Winehouse 26th.

EARLY YEARS

Amy Jade Winehouse was born to Jewish parents on September 14, 1983, at Chase Farm Hospital in Gordon Hill, Enfield. Her mother, Janis Winehouse (née Seaton), was a pharmacist; her father, Mitchell "Mitch" Winehouse, was a window panel installer and cab driver. In 2003, her mother received a multiple sclerosis diagnosis.

Harris Winehouse, Winehouse's great-great-grandfather, moved to London in 1891 from Minsk, Belarus. Alex, who was born in 1979, was her older brother. She went to Osidge Primary School and Ashmole School for her senior education while growing up in the Southgate neighborhood of London. When Winehouse was a young girl, she attended a Jewish Sunday school. In a post-game interview, she showed her disdain for the school by claiming that she used to beg her father to let her stay home instead and that attending the school had taught her nothing about being Jewish. Winehouse claimed in the same interview that she only ever visited a synagogue on Yom Kippur "out of respect".

Many of Winehouse's maternal uncles were jazz musicians in the industry. Amy's maternal grandmother Cynthia had dated English jazz saxophonist Ronnie Scott and had been a singer. She and Amy's parents had an impact on Amy's jazz inclinations. When she was disciplined at school, she would sing "Fly Me to the Moon" before going up to the headmistress to be warned off. Her father, Mitch, frequently sang Frank Sinatra songs to her. After her parents divorced when she was nine years old,

Winehouse split her time between living with her mother in Whetstone, London, and her father and his girlfriend in Hatfield Heath, Essex.

Amy's grandma Cynthia recommended that she enroll in the Susi Earnshaw Theatre School in 1992. Amy went there on Saturdays to enhance her tap dancing and vocal training. Before enrolling full-time at Sylvia Young Theatre School, she attended the school for four years and co-founded the short-lived rap trio Sweet 'n' Sour with her childhood friend Juliette Ashby. Later, it was said that Winehouse had been expelled at the age of 14 for "not applying herself" and for having her nose pierced, but Sylvia Young refuted this, saying: "She changed schools at 15...Despite what I've heard, she wasn't expelled. I would never have dismissed Amy".

Auch Mitch Winehouse disputed the allegations.

Amy's Sylvia Young Theatre School English instructor recalled her as a talented writer and predicted that she would go on to become a novelist or journalist. At age 16, she left the BRIT School in Selhurst, Croydon, where she had previously attended the Mount School in Mill Hill.

When Winehouse was 14 years old, she got her guitar after playing around with her brother Alex before starting to write music. Soon after, she started earning a living by writing about entertainment for the World Entertainment News Network and singing with the Bolsha

Band, a local band. She joined the National Youth Jazz Orchestra in July 2000 and soon rose to the position of a featured female vocalist. Sarah Vaughan and Dinah Washington, the latter of whom she was already listening to at home, influenced her. Tyler James, a soul performer who is Winehouse's best friend, delivered her demo tape to an A&R representative.

CAREER

CAREER START-UP (2002–05)

Winehouse was paid £250 per week against potential earnings when she joined Simon Fuller's 19 Management in 2002. Winehouse kept a recording industry secret while she was being groomed by the management firm, even though she often sang jazz classics at the Cobden Club. When the manager of the Lewinson Brothers showed him some recordings of his clients, which featured Winehouse as the lead vocalist, Darcus Beese, her future A&R representative at Island, then learned about her. The management informed him that he was not permitted to reveal who the vocalist was when he inquired. After deciding he wanted to sign her, Beese spent months inquiring around until he finally found out who the singer was. But by this point, Winehouse had already cut a handful of tracks and agreed to a publication deal with EMI. She also met producer Salaam Remi through these record labels, which was helpful for her career.

Beese presented Winehouse to Nick Gatfield, his supervisor, and the Island head was excited to sign the young musician. Winehouse was signed to Island, even though EMI and Virgin officials had begun to show interest in the singer. According to Beese, who spoke to HitQuarters, the popularity of a performer who was an unusual pop sensation at the time was brought on by a backlash against reality TV music shows, which featured consumers desperate for new, sincere young talent.

Frank, Winehouse's debut album, was made available on October 20, 2003. Apart from two covers, Winehouse co-wrote every song on the album, which was primarily produced by Salaam Remi and featured numerous jazz-inspired tunes. The "cool, critical gaze" in the lyrics of the album was praised, garnering positive reviews. Winehouse's voice was compared to others like Macy Gray and Sarah Vaughan.

When it was nominated for the Brit Awards in the categories of British Female Solo Artist and British Urban Act in 2004, the album rose to the top of the UK Albums Chart. Later, it sold platinum amounts. She and Remi won the Ivor Novello Award for Best Contemporary Song later that year for their debut joint hit, "Stronger Than Me." Additionally, the album made the Mercury Music Prize 2004 shortlist. She had performances at the V Festival, Montreal International Jazz Festival, and Glastonbury Festival - Jazz World that same year. Winehouse stated that she was "only 80% behind the album" after its release because Island Records disregarded her recommendations for the tracks and mixes to be used. "Take the Box," "In My Bed"/"You Sent Me Flying," and "Pumps"/"Help Yourself" were further hits from the album.

INTERNATIONAL SUCCESS (2006–08)

After releasing her debut album with jazz influences, Amy Winehouse began to concentrate on the girl groups of the 1950s and 1960s. Winehouse enlisted the Dap-Kings, Sharon Jones' longtime backing group from New York, to accompany her on stage and in the studio.

In Amy, My Daughter, Mitch Winehouse describes how intriguing it was to observe her creative process: her studio perfectionism and the way she would record her songs on a CD and play them in his cab outside to get a sense of how most people would hear them.

On Mark Ronson's New York radio program on East Village Radio in May 2006, Winehouse's demo versions of songs including "You Know I'm No Good" and "Rehab" were played. Both of these tracks were supposed to feature on her second album and were among the first brand-new songs to be played on the radio following the release of "Pumps." Salaam Remi and Ronson, who each contributed equally to the creation of the 11-track album, finished it in just five months. In a 2010 interview, Ronson claimed that one of the reasons he liked working with Winehouse was because she was direct when she didn't like his work. She believed he was a sound engineer when they first met, whereas she had anticipated an older man with a beard.

Back to Black was quickly promoted, and early in October 2006 Winehouse's official website was revamped with a new design and previews of unheard music. The UK saw the release of Back to Black on October 30, 2006. In January 2007, it spent two weeks at the top of the UK Albums Chart before falling and then rising for many weeks in February. It debuted in the US at position 7 on the Billboard 200. In the UK, it was the best-selling album of 2007, selling 1.85 million copies overall. The Ronson-produced song "Rehab" served as the album's first single. In both the US and the UK, the song peaked at number ten. "Rehab" was selected as the Best Song of 2007 by Time magazine.

Josh Tyrangiel, a writer, lauded Winehouse for her self-assurance, stating that "it's impossible not to be seduced by her originality" and that "she is mouthy, funny, sultry, and quite possibly crazy." The production by Mark Ronson, which alludes to four decades worth of soul music without ever plagiarizing it, makes it the finest song of 2007.

"You Know I'm No Good," the second single from the album and the album's lead single in the US, was released in January 2007 with a remix that included Ghostface Killah's rap vocals. In the end, it peaked at position 18 on the UK singles chart. Released in the UK in April 2007 and reaching its highest position at number 25, the title single, "Back to Black," was more popular in mainland Europe. The single releases of "Tears Dry on Their Own" and "Love Is a Losing Game" did not have the same level of popularity.

On November 5, 2007, Back to Black received a deluxe edition in the UK. The bonus disc includes "Valerie" as well as B-sides, out-of-print, and live songs. I Told You I Was Trouble: Live in London, Winehouse's first DVD was released on the same day in the UK and on November 13 in the US. Along with a 50-minute documentary tracing the singer's career over the past four years, it also features a live performance from London's Shepherd's Bush Empire. On November 20, 2007, Frank was released in the US to rave reviews. The album debuted on the Billboard 200 chart at position 61.

Along with working on her record, she also co-wrote tracks with other musicians. The vocalist for the song "Valerie" on Ronson's solo album Version was Winehouse. When it was released as a single in October, the song reached its UK peak at number two. The British Single of the Year 2008 Brit Award nomination for "Valerie" was announced. "B Boy Baby", her collaboration with ex-Sugababe Mutya Buena, was published on December 17, 2007. It was the fourth single from Real Girl, Buena's debut album. Additionally, Winehouse and Missy Elliott discussed collaborating on her album Block Party.

Late in 2006, Winehouse performed in front of large crowds to promote the release of Back to Black, including a Little Noise Sessions benefit event at the Union Chapel in London's Islington. Winehouse, Paul Weller, and Holland's Rhythm and Blues Orchestra covered Marvin Gaye's "I Heard It Through the Grapevine" on his show Jools Holland's Annual

Hootenanny on December 31, 2006. She also sang "Monkey Man" by Toots and the Maytals. Before Winehouse performed "Rehab" at the 2007 MTV Movie Awards in Universal City, California, on June 3, 2007, he asked actor Bruce Willis to introduce her. She gave performances at several festivals throughout the summer of 2007, including the Chicago Lollapalooza and the Glastonbury Festival.

However, the remainder of her tour did not go as well. At the National Indoor Arena in Birmingham in November 2007, the first night of a 17-date tour was disrupted by boos and walkouts. A Birmingham Mail critic referred to it as "one of the saddest nights of my life...I saw a supremely talented artist reduced to tears, stumbling around the stage and, unforgivably, swearing at the audience." Other performances came to a similar end; for instance, during her London performance at the Hammersmith Apollo, fans remarked that she "looked highly intoxicated throughout," but on November 27, 2007, she announced that she would no longer be making any public appearances or performing, citing the recommendation of her doctor to take a complete break. The decision was attributed to "the rigors of touring and the intense emotional strain that Amy has been under in recent weeks," according to a statement from concert promoter Live Nation. Her anxiety before public performances was discussed by Mitch Winehouse in his 2012 book, Amy, My Daughter. For the third week in a row, Back to Black was at the top of the Billboard Pan European charts on January 13, 2008.

Winehouse won five Grammy Awards on February 10, 2008: Record of the Year, Song of the Year, Best Female Pop Vocal Performance for the song "Rehab," and Best Pop Vocal Album. The singer also received a Grammy for Best New Artist, putting her on the list of British female acts with the most Grammy awards in 2009, according to the Guinness Book of Records.

Back to Black was also a candidate for Album of the Year. She collaborated with Ronson on the non-classical album that took home the Grammy Award for Producer of the Year. In allusion to the 2008 Camden Market fire, she said, "This is for London because Camden Town ain't burning down," as she concluded her acceptance speech for Record of the Year. She couldn't attend the ceremony in Los Angeles because her visa approval was delayed, so she performed "You Know I'm No Good" and "Rehab" via satellite at 3 a.m. UK time.

Back to Black initially peaked at number seven on the US Billboard 200, but after the Grammys, album sales surged, propelling it to number two. Winehouse sang "Valerie" with Mark Ronson at the 2008 Brit Awards at Earls Court in London on February 20, 2008, and then sang "Love Is a Losing Game" afterward. She pleaded with the crowd to "make some noise for my Blake." Back to Black's special deluxe version peaked at number one on the UK album charts on March 2. Frank debuted at number 35 on the charts, while the original edition of the album peaked at number 30 in its 68th week on the charts.

She gave a "well-executed 40-minute" concert in Paris in early March at the opening of a Fendi store, according to reports. A total of 2,467,575 copies of the album had been sold as of March 12; 318,350 of those copies had been sold in the ten weeks prior, landing it for the first time in the UK's list of the ten best-selling albums of the twenty-first century. Back to Black topped the pan-European charts on April 7 for the sixth consecutive week and thirteenth overall. On April 14, 2008, a 78-minute DVD titled Amy Winehouse: The Girl Done Good: A Documentary Review was made available. Interviews with people who knew her when she was young, those who assisted in her career, jazz music experts, and music and pop culture experts are included in the documentary.

Winehouse was the first artist to ever win two nominations for the top prize, Best Song Musically & Lyrically, at the 2008 Ivor Novello Awards in May. She was nominated for "You Know I'm No Good" and won the prize for "Love Is a Losing Game". The 2006 Novello Award winner for best current song "Rehab" was also nominated in 2008 for best-selling British single. Winehouse was also a nominee for the Act of the Year category at the 2008 MTV Europe Music Awards.

Winehouse appeared at the Rock in Rio Lisboa festival in Portugal in May 2008 despite reportedly being discouraged from doing so by her father, manager, and different members of her touring team. The audience warmed up to her despite her voice issues and late arrival throughout the set. She also played two Specials covers in addition to her original songs. On June 27, 2008, Winehouse performed in a concert honoring Nelson Mandela's 90th birthday in London's Hyde Park. The following day, she appeared at the Glastonbury Festival. She had a well-received 50-minute performance on July 12 at the Oxegen Festival in Ireland; the following day, she played a 14-song set at T in the Park.

She performed at the V Festival's Staffordshire leg on August 16 before performing at the festival's Chelmsford leg the next day. According to the organizers, Winehouse drew the festival's largest crowds. Mixed feedback from the audience was received. On September 6, she performed as the Saturday headlining act at Bestival. Her performance was praised for being polished; nevertheless, it was cut short by a curfew since Winehouse began her set an hour late and by her storming off stage.

The Rock and Roll Hall of Fame Annex NYC, which opened in December 2008, featured a section called "Roots and Influences" that examined the relationships between various musicians and featured a sample of Winehouse's music. One line of conversation began with Billie Holiday, went on to include Mary J. Blige and Aretha Franklin, and ended with Amy Winehouse.

The seventh-best-selling album worldwide in 2008 was Back to Black. Because of the album's sales, Universal Music's recorded music sector did not endure a decline in market performance comparable to that of the whole music industry.

FINAL PROJECTS BEFORE DEATH (2009–11)

One-fifth of respondents in a 2009 Harris Interactive survey of Americans for VisitBritain said they had listened to Amy Winehouse's music in the year prior. She collaborated with Rhythms del Mundo on their rendition of "Cupid" by Sam Cooke for an Artists Project Earth charity CD that was released in July of that same year.

In November 2010, the Quincy Jones tribute album Q Soul Bossa Nostra was published. Winehouse and Ronson contributed a cover of Lesley Gore's "It's My Party" to the album. She had agreed to join a group with Questlove of the Roots, but their collaboration was delayed by her difficulties getting a visa. As part of the collaboration, Salaam Remi and Winehouse had previously produced some content. The Times claims that in 2008, Universal Music demanded new material from her even though, as of 2 September, she had not been in the vicinity of a recording studio. Winehouse's spokesperson was quoted as saying that she had not been given a timetable for finishing her third album, for which she was learning to play the drums, at the end of October.

Winehouse resumed her performance at a jazz event in Saint Lucia in May 2009 despite torrential rain and technological issues. She reportedly had problems recalling songs and was shaky on her feet during her performance. She apologized to the audience for being "bored" and cut off the performance midway through a song. But while she was in Saint

Lucia, she collaborated with Remi on some brand-new music. Winehouse performed at the V Festival with the Specials on their songs "You're Wondering Now" and "Ghost Town" on August 23, that year.

According to Island, a new album would be released in 2010. Darcus Beese, the co-president of the island, stated, "I've heard a couple of song demos that have floored me." According to a July 2010 report, Winehouse's next album would be released no later than January 2011. She said, "It's going to be very much the same as my second album, where there's a lot of jukebox stuff and songs that are... just jukebox." However, Ronson said at the time that he had not yet begun the album's recording. She and Ronson sang "Valerie" during a movie premiere, but she didn't remember all of the lyrics. Winehouse gave a four-song show in October to support her clothing company. She performed a 40-minute concert in Moscow in December 2010 for a party hosted by a Russian businessman, who personally chose the music.

Janelle Monáe and Mayer Hawthorne served as the opening acts for Winehouse's five performances in Brazil in January 2011. The audience in Dubai booed her during the performance the next month, so she ended it early. During the performance, Winehouse was reportedly drowsy, unfocused, and "tipsy".

Belgrade served as the launch point for Winehouse's 12-city European tour on June 18, 2011. Her performance was dubbed a scandal and a disaster by the local media, and she was booed off the stage because she was allegedly too inebriated to perform. Winehouse's performances were deemed "a huge shame and a disappointment" by Serbian Minister of Defense Dragan Utanovac. She reportedly couldn't recall the name of her band, the lyrics to her songs, or the location of the city she was in. Winehouse allegedly sought to leave the stage but was prevented from doing so by her security, who compelled her to perform. The following week's scheduled appearances in Istanbul and Athens were subsequently canceled by her. On June 21, it was revealed that she has postponed all of her tour dates and will have "as long as it takes" to get her act together.

On July 20, 2011, Winehouse made her final public appearance at Camden's Roundhouse, where she unexpectedly appeared on stage to support her goddaughter Dionne Bromfield, who was performing "Mama Said" with the Wanted. Three days later Winehouse passed away. For American singer Tony Bennett's album Duets II, which was released on September 20, 2011, she recorded a duet with him. To honor her 28th birthday, their album's lead track, "Body and Soul," was made available on MTV and VH1 on September 14, 2011.

PRIVATE LIFE

Despite not being religious, Winehouse claimed satisfaction in being reared as a Jew. Winehouse frequently performed with a huge Star of David medallion and stated in an interview that "being Jewish to me is about being together as a real family. It's not about lighting candles and saying bracha."

The Jewish Museum London held an exhibition named "Amy Winehouse: A Family Portrait" in 2013 to honor Winehouse. Her paternal great-great-grandfather's arrival from Minsk in 1890 and how the family ultimately made their way to London were both investigated by the museum. The family initially worked in working-class positions before gradually transitioning to middle-class jobs.

In addition to the phrase "Daddy's Girl" on her left arm in honor of her father and the image of a pin-up girl with the name "Cynthia" on her right arm in honor of her Jewish grandmother, Winehouse is believed to have had 14 tattoos.

RELATIONSHIPS

While on a break from her on-and-off boyfriend and future husband, Blake Fielder-Civil, Winehouse dated musician-chef, Alex Clare. She and Clare shared a short period in residence, and in a move that Fielder-Civil would later duplicate, Clare sold the News of the World his story, which was then published under the headline "Bondage Crazed Amy Just Can't Beehive in Bed."

Fielder-Civil, a former assistant in video production, left Bourne Grammar School at age 16 and relocated from his native Lincolnshire to London. On May 18, 2007, in Miami Beach, Florida, he wed Winehouse. After drinking, Winehouse acknowledged in a June 2007 interview, "If he says one thing I don't like, then I'll chin him."

In August 2007, they were photographed in the streets of London bloodied and bruised after an alleged fight, though she claimed her injuries were self-inflicted. Parents and in-laws of Winehouse have openly expressed their many worries, with the latter claiming worries that the two would commit suicide. Fielder-Civil's father urged supporters to avoid Winehouse's music, but Mitch Winehouse insisted that doing so would not be beneficial. According to Fielder-Civil, he introduced Winehouse to crack cocaine and heroin, according to a British tabloid report. Fielder-Civil reportedly revealed that he and Winehouse would cut themselves to lessen the discomfort of withdrawal during a visit with Winehouse at the prison in July 2008.

Fielder-Civil was detained from 21 July 2008 to 25 February 2009 as a result of his guilty plea to charges of attempting to tamper with the course of justice and causing great bodily damage with intent. He attacked a pub owner in July 2007 and shattered the victim's cheek in the process. The landlord testified that the £200,000 he received as part of a contract to "effectively throw the court case and not turn up" belonged to Winehouse, but she skipped a meeting with the guys engaged in the conspiracy to go to an awards ceremony, according to the prosecution. As the financial manager for his daughter, Mitch Winehouse has denied that she was responsible for the payoff.

Winehouse claimed that her "whole marriage was based on doing drugs" and that "for the time being I've just forgotten I'm even married" when she was seen with aspiring actor Josh Bowman on vacation in Saint Lucia in early January 2009. On January 12, Winehouse's spokesman confirmed that "papers have been received" for what Fielder-Civil's solicitor claimed were divorce proceedings based on a claim of adultery. Winehouse was quoted in a magazine in March as saying, "I still love Blake and I want him to move into my new house with me—that was my plan all along... I won't let him divorce me. He's the male version of me and we're perfect for each other."

However, an uncontested divorce was granted on 16 July 2009 and was made official on 28 August 2009. In the settlement, Fielder-Civil did not get any money.

From early 2010 until her passing, she was dating Reg Traviss, a British screenwriter and filmmaker. Media claims and a biography published by Winehouse's father claim that Traviss and Winehouse had been engaged and were expecting a child.

Pete Doherty said that he and Winehouse had once been lovers after Winehouse's passing. To the question about her relationship with Doherty posed by Rolling Stone reporter Claire Hoffman in July 2008, Winehouse responded, "We're just good friends," adding, "I asked Pete to do a concept EP, and he made this face, and he looked at me like I'd pooped on the floor. He wouldn't do it. We're just really close."

ALCOHOLISM AND MENTAL ILLNESS

Media coverage of Winehouse's struggles with substance misuse was extensive. She underwent a period of severe drinking, drug usage, and weight loss in 2005. People who saw her at the close of that year and the beginning of 2006 stated that she had recovered about the time when Back to Black was written. Her family feels that her addiction began as a result of the mid-2006 passing of her grandmother, who served as a calming force in her life. Winehouse postponed several performances in the UK and Europe in August 2007, citing fatigue and poor health. During this time, she was hospitalized for what was described as a heroin, ecstasy, cocaine, ketamine, and alcohol overdose. She acknowledged having issues with self-harm, depression, and eating disorders in several interviews.

Soon after, Winehouse's father remarked that when he had made public statements regarding her problems he was using the media because it seemed to be the only way to get through to her. Winehouse had previously claimed that the drugs were to blame for her hospitalization and that "I thought that it was over for me then." Winehouse claimed that she was manic depressive and not an alcoholic in an interview with The Album Chart Show on British television, noting that this sounded like "an alcoholic in denial." Winehouse, according to a US reporter, was a "victim of mental illness in a society that doesn't understand or respond to mental illness with great effectiveness."

According to Winehouse's representative in December 2007, the singer was in a program under the supervision of a doctor and was using music composition as a way to cope with her problems. A woman, allegedly Winehouse, is seen in a video posted by the British magazine The Sun appearing to smoke crack cocaine and admitting to using ecstasy and valium.

Winehouse's father moved in with her, and her record label, Island Records, announced the cancellation of preparations for a promotional campaign in the United States on her behalf. The Metropolitan Police received the footage on January 23, 2008, and on February 5, they questioned the woman. No accusations were made. Winehouse reportedly checked herself into a rehab center at the end of January for a two-week therapy course. Winehouse's spokesman stated on March 26 that she was "doing well". According to her record label, her rehabilitation was still tenuous. By late April 2008, there was concern that she had failed to recover from her drug use due to her unpredictable behavior, which included an assault allegation. Then, Winehouse's father and manager requested her detention under the 1983 Mental Health Act. Her unkempt demeanor before, during, and following a planned club night in September 2008 sparked fresh rumors of a relapse. She looked to have cuts on her arms and legs, according to photographers, who were cited in reports.

Her doctor claims that Winehouse stopped using illicit drugs in 2008. Winehouse stated in an interview from October 2010 that she decided to stop using drugs because "I woke up one day and was like, 'I don't want to do this anymore.'" However, alcohol consumption became an issue for Winehouse after she abstained for a few weeks. According to her doctor, Winehouse had psychological and psychiatric assessments in 2010 and was prescribed Librium for alcohol withdrawal and anxiety. She also declined psychological counseling.

VIOLENCE AND DIFFICULTY WITH THE LAW

Winehouse acknowledged in 2006 that she had punched a female fan in the face after she had criticized her for marrying Blake Fielder-Civil. She then attacked her husband, kneeing him in the groin as he tried to calm her down. Winehouse and Fielder-Civil were detained in Bergen, Norway, in October 2007 for possessing seven grams of marijuana. The pair were later freed after paying a 3850 kroner (about £350) fine. Winehouse first filed an appeal against the fines but eventually withdrew it.

Winehouse was issued a warning on April 26, 2008, after confessing to police that she had slapped a 38-year-old man in the face, the first of two "common assault" offenses she would commit. She turned herself in freely and was detained for the night. Police claimed that she was "in no fit state" to be interviewed when she arrived.

After a video showing Winehouse appearing to be smoking crack cocaine was given to the police in January, she was detained on suspicion of narcotics possession ten days later but freed on bail a short time later because it was impossible to determine what she was inhaling from the video. When the Crown Prosecution Service was unable to prove that the substance in the video was a restricted narcotic, it considered charging her but ultimately decided against it. A few lawmakers responded adversely. Following that, two Londoners were accused of conspiring to give cocaine and ecstasy to Winehouse. On

December 13, 2008, one of the two received a two-year community order while the other received a two-year prison sentence.

Following a claim by dancer Sherene Flash that Winehouse struck her in the eye at the September 2008 Prince's Trust charity night, Winehouse was detained and charged with common assault on March 5, 2009. Due to the new legal matter, Winehouse's spokesperson confirmed that the singer would not be performing at the US Coachella Festival. Winehouse appeared in court on March 17 to enter her not-guilty plea. Beginning on July 23, the prosecution's case against Winehouse alleged that she used "deliberate and unjustifiable violence" while pretending to be under the influence of alcohol or another drug. She claimed in court that she did not punch

Flash but rather sought to push her away out of fear; she gave as reasons her fear that Flash would sell her tale to a tabloid, her concern about Flash's height, and Flash's "rude" behavior. District Judge Timothy Workman concluded on July 24 that Winehouse was not guilty, citing the facts that all but two of the witnesses were drunk at the time of the event and that the medical evidence did not demonstrate "the sort of injury that often occurs when there is a forceful punch to the eye."

Winehouse was detained for a third time on December 19, 2009, after allegedly hitting the Milton Keynes Theatre's front-of-house manager after being asked to leave her seat. She was also charged with a new public order offense. Winehouse was given a conditional discharge after entering a guilty plea to the charges.

PAPARAZZI

Under the Protection from Harassment Act of 1997, Winehouse won an injunction against a prominent paparazzi agency, Big Pictures, to prevent them from following her. The High Court subsequently imposed a court order prohibiting their pursuit of her in 2009. Additionally, it was forbidden for photographers to follow Winehouse within 100 meters of her London home or take pictures of her inside or at the houses of her friends and family. A media article quoted individuals close to the singer as saying that legal action was launched out of fear for Winehouse's safety and the protection of those close to her.

MEDICAL ISSUES

Earlier assertions by Mitch Winehouse that his daughter had early-stage emphysema were incorrect, and Winehouse's publicist clarified this on June 23, 2008, saying instead that she showed symptoms of what could eventually cause emphysema.

Additionally, according to Mitch Winehouse, his daughter had an abnormal heartbeat and lungs that were only functioning at 70% of their potential. He claimed that her habitual usage of crack cocaine was to blame for these issues. Additionally, according to the singer's father, physicians had informed Amy Winehouse that if she continued to use crack cocaine, she would need to wear an oxygen mask and eventually pass away. According to Mitch

Winehouse, the singer was responding "fabulously" to treatment, which included wearing nicotine patches, in a radio interview. According to Keith Prowse, spokesman for the British Lung Foundation, this kind of illness is treatable.

Norman H. Edelman of the American Lung Association explained that if she stopped smoking, her lung functions would decline at the rate of a normal person, but continued smoking would lead to a more rapid decline in lung function. Prowse added that the condition was not normal for a person her age but that "heavy smoking and inhaling other substances like drugs can age the lungs prematurely."

After returning from a brief leave of absence to sing at Nelson Mandela's 90th birthday and a concert in Glastonbury, Winehouse was discharged from the London Clinic 24 hours later and continued undergoing treatment as an outpatient. Winehouse revealed in July 2008 that she had been given a diagnosis of "some areas of emphysema" and claimed to be getting better by "eating loads of healthy food, sleeping loads, playing my guitar, making music, and writing letters to my husband every day." She also kept a vertical tanning bed in her apartment.

On October 25, 2008, Winehouse checked her lungs and chest as a precaution at the London Clinic for what was thought to be a chest infection. Winehouse frequently entered and exited the facility and was allowed to choose her home leave schedule. On November 23, 2008, she went back to the hospital because of a reported drug response.

DEATH

Winehouse's security claimed that when he had visited her home three days before her passing, he had noticed that she appeared to be a little buzzed. She had been "laughing, listening to music and watching TV at 2 a.m. the day of her death," according to him, who saw moderate drinking over the following several days. At 10 a.m. On July 23, 2011, at 05:00 BST, he saw her laying in bed and tried unsuccessfully to wake her. She typically slept in late after a night out, so this did not raise many red flags. The bodyguard claimed that shortly after 3 o'clock, he checked on her again and discovered that she was still lying in the same posture as before. He claimed that after performing another check, he discovered that she had no pulse and no sign of respiration. He claimed that he then dialed emergency services. Two ambulances arrived at Winehouse's Camden, London, home at 3:54 p.m. At the site, Winehouse's death was confirmed. The Metropolitan Police quickly announced that she had passed away. Her death at the age of 27 generated comparisons in the media to other musicians who passed away at the same age, known as the 27 Club.

Following the news of her passing, media and camera teams showed up, and mourners gathered close to Winehouse's home. One little and two large bottles of vodka were found in her chamber when forensic experts entered the apartment while police blocked off the street outside. The singer's second Guinness World Record, for the most songs by a woman to simultaneously chart on the UK singles chart, was broken after her passing with eight tracks.

A misadventure verdict was rendered during a coroner's inquest. According to the study that was made public on October 26, 2011, Winehouse had a blood alcohol content of 416 mg per 100 ml (0.416%) at the time of her death, which is more than five times the legal limit for driving after drinking. The coroner stated that "the unintended consequence of such potentially fatal levels was her sudden death."

Many musicians have since paid tribute to Winehouse, including U2, M.I.A., Lady Gaga, Marianne Faithfull, Ronnie Spector, Bruno Mars, Nicki Minaj, Keisha Buchanan, Rihanna, George Michael, Adele, Kelly Clarkson, Courtney Love, and the rock group Green Day, who wrote a song in her honor titled "Song in Her Honor."

Winehouse's record label, Universal Republic, issued a statement that read in part: "We Patti Smith, a singer, included the Amy Winehouse tribute song "This Is the Girl" in her 2012 album Banga."

Winehouse did not make a will; her inheritance was inherited by her parents. Mark Ronson dedicated his UK number-one album Uptown Special to Winehouse, stating: "I'm always thinking of you and inspired by you." The Amy Winehouse Foundation was founded by Winehouse's parents to protect young people from the devastation caused by drug abuse; Winehouse's brother Alex works there.

British officials restarted their investigation into Winehouse's death on December 17, 2012.

A second inquest, held on January 8, 2013, affirmed that Winehouse had overdosed on alcohol unintentionally. Alex Winehouse stated in a June 2013 interview that he thought his sister's eating issue and the resulting physical frailty were the main factors in her demise:

She had severe bulimia symptoms. That isn't exactly a revelation; you could tell by looking at her. The way she was going, she would have eventually passed away, but her bulimia was what ultimately did her in. I believe that made her weaker and more prone. She would have been physically stronger if she had not suffered from an eating disorder.

FUNERAL

On July 26, 2011, a private funeral for Winehouse was held at Edgwarebury Lane Cemetery in North London. Those present at the private service conducted by Rabbi Frank Hellner included her mother and father, Janis and Mitch Winehouse, close friends Nick Grimshaw and Kelly Osbourne, producer Mark Ronson, goddaughter Dionne Bromfield, and her boyfriend Reg Traviss. Carole King's "So Far Away" completed the funeral, with mourners joining in on the singing. Her father gave the eulogy, saying, "Goodnight, my angel, sleep tight. Mummy and Daddy love you ever so much." At Golders Green Crematorium, she was later cremated. The family intended to observe Shiva for two days. At Edgwarebury Lane Cemetery on September 16, 2012,

Winehouse's ashes were interred next to those of her grandmother, Cynthia Levy.

HONORS AND LEGACY

SCULPTURE AND TRIBUTES

In May 2008, the Mall Galleries in London unveiled an exhibition that featured a sculpture of Winehouse called Excess. Guy Portelli's artwork featured a small image of the singer resting on top of a broken champagne bottle with a pool of liquid underneath. One outstretched hand held a glass, and the torso was coated in what looked to be tiny tablets. The same exhibition featured another work, a print by Charlotte Suckling titled Celebrity 1.

On July 23, 2008, a wax replica of Winehouse was put on display at the Madame Tussauds in London. The singer's parents were present during the event, but not her. The Only Good

Rock Star Is a Dead Rock Star by Marco Perego, which depicts Amy Winehouse with an apple in her hand and a bullet hole in her head after being shot by Beat poet and American author William S. Burroughs (in a recreation of the unintentional killing of his wife Joan Vollmer), was slated to open in New York's Half Gallery on November 14 and sell for $100,000. According to Perego, "Rock stars are the sacrificial animals of society." A representative for Winehouse said: "It's a funny type of tribute. The artist seems to be controlled by a false Amy from the tabloids. Many people market their products using her appearance."

Winehouse was among the British cultural celebrities Sir Peter Blake chose in 2012 to feature on a new rendition of his most well-known piece of art, the Beatles' Sgt.

Pepper's Lonely Hearts Club Band album cover, to honor the British cultural icons he most admires.

A statue of Winehouse, made by sculptor Scott Eaton, was unveiled at Stables Market in Camden Town, north London, on September 14, 2014, the day before her 31st birthday. The ceremony took place at Camden's Stable Market, where it will serve as a perpetual tribute to her. After meeting Winehouse's father Mitch, the monument was created by London-based Eaton, who described it as an attempt to reflect her "attitude and strength, but also give subtle hints of insecurity."

"Now Amy will forever watch the comings and goings of her hometown," her father Mitch remarked of the statue. Amy was in love with

Camden, which is where her international followers associate her with.

'Amy's Glance,' a picture of the singer by artist Dan Llywelyn Hall, was displayed at The London Art Fair in 2018.

Winehouse's parents, Mitch and Janis, were present as a stone bearing her name was unveiled in Camden's new Music Walk of Fame in March 2020.

RECOGNITION AND NOMINATIONS

Winehouse received a nomination for a Brit Award for Best British Female Solo Artist, an Ivor Novello Award from the British Academy of Songwriters for Best Contemporary Song ("Stronger Than Me"), and inclusion in Robert Dimery's 2006 book, 1001 Albums You Must Hear Before You Die.

Back to Black, her second studio album, received numerous nominations, including two Brit Awards (Best British Album and Best British Female Solo Artist), six Grammy Awards (including five wins), four Ivor Novello Awards, four MTV Europe Music Awards, three MTV Video Music Awards, three World Music Awards, and nominations for the Mercury Prize

(Album of the Year) and a MOBO Awards (Best UK Female). It was also nominated for the Mercury Prize and the MOBO Awards. Winehouse had 60 nominations for the 23 prizes she won over her career.

CRITICAL EVALUATION

Winehouse was renowned for her rich, expressive contralto voice and her diverse mix of musical genres, which included jazz, rhythm, and blues, soul (also known as "blue-eyed soul," "neo-soul," and "soul"), and soul.

Winehouse was said to be "the preeminent vocal talent of her generation" by Garry Mulholland of the BBC. She was one of the top vocalists in the UK in the 2000s, according to Cyril Cordor of AllMusic; "fans and critics alike embraced her rugged charm, brash sense of humor, and distinctively soulful and jazzy vocals." Caroline Sullivan subsequently stated in The Guardian that "her idolization of Dinah Washington and the Ronettes distinguished her from nearly all newly-minted pop singers of the early 2000s; her exceptionally-susceptible-to-heartbreak voice did the rest."

Soon after Amy Winehouse passed away, several well-known commentators evaluated her legacy: Sasha Frere-Jones of The New Yorker proclaimed, "Nobody can match Winehouse's unique transitions or her utterly weird phrasings. When she was on, Winehouse had few peers. She wasn't an octave-jumper like other big divas of the moment, but her contralto had a snap to it that enriched even the simplest syllables with a full spectrum of emotion."

She had a sound reminiscent of a classic 1960s soul singer who emerged in an environment devoid of boundaries. But now that unrestrained traditionalism is in charge, her lovely addendum has been condensed. Through artists like Janelle Monáe, Erykah Badu, and Jill Scott, the American soul has advanced. Winehouse, however, was a good shepherd in the past.

For his part, Robert Christgau criticized Winehouse as "a self-aggrandizing self-abuser who's taken seriously because she makes a show of soul" The vocalist "simulated gravitas by running her suicidal tendencies through an amalgam of 20th-century African-American vocal stylings—the slides, growls, and melismatic outcries that for many mature are now the only reliable signifiers of pop substance," according to him.

On VH1's list of the 100 Greatest Women in Music, Winehouse was ranked 26th on February 13, 2012. Singer-songwriter Bob Dylan referred to Amy Winehouse as "the last real individualist around" in March 2017 while praising her final album, Back to Black.

IMAGE

Winehouse was influenced by and modeled her style after soul-girl groups like the Ronettes.

In the 1960s female groups were Winehouse's greatest love. Her "instantly recognizable" beehive hairstyle (a weave) was taken from her hairdresser, Alex Foden, and her Cleopatra makeup was taken from the Ronettes. It could be argued that Ronnie Spector, who performed with her fellow Ronettes at the Brooklyn Fox Theater more than 40 years ago, all but invented Winehouse's style in the first place, was so taken aback by a photograph of Winehouse in the New York Post that she exclaimed, "I don't know her, I never met her, and when I saw that pic, I thought, 'That's me!'" Then I realized, "No, it's Amy!" I wasn't wearing my glasses.

74

Guy Trebay, a style reporter for the New York Times, talked about how Winehouse's style was influenced by many different people after she passed away. In the words of Trebay, "Her stylish husband, Blake Fielder-Civil, may have influenced her look." In addition, Trebay noticed:

She was a 5-foot-3 visual reference book, most notably to Ronnie Spector of The Ronettes, but also to white British soul singer Mari Wilson, who was better known for her beehive than her voice; to punk god Johnny Thunders; to the fierce council-house chicks; and to a long line of bad girls, including Salt-n-Pepa and irresistible man traps who always seemed to meet the same tragic end.

Joe Levy, a former editor of Rolling Stone, described her appearance in further detail as follows:

Her style was a savvy mosaic, just like her best work, which used sampling to create aural licks and stylistic snippets from Motown, Stax, punk, and early hip-hop. If you were heading downtown and turned left in the 1990s, every girl would have looked like Bettie Page. However, they didn't combine Bettie Page and Brigitte Bardot with a tiny bit of Ronnie Spector as Amy Winehouse did.

When Winehouse visited Miami to collaborate with Salaam Remi on Back to Black, she was inspired by the Latinas she saw there to apply bold red lipstick, full eyebrows, and heavy eyeliner. The British tabloids regularly disparaged her appearance.

In addition to being nominated for "Best Solo Artist" and "Best Music DVD" at the 2008 NME Awards, Winehouse also won "Worst Dressed Performer" honors. The 48th annual "Ten Worst Dressed Women" list by Richard Blackwell placed Winehouse second, just behind Victoria Beckham.

INFLUENCE

Winehouse's success, according to Adele, helped to make her and Duffy's trip to the United States "a bit smoother." Winehouse paved the door for atypical women to achieve mainstream musical success, according to Lady Gaga, who said that this helped her climb the charts. Those who sought to pull off a marketing coup produced Amy Winehouse, according to Raphael Saadiq, Anthony Hamilton, and John Legend. The fact that it reintroduced this music to some listeners and served as an introduction to others is a plus. Getting past the vintage element, gave the genre new life.

Bruno Mars, Tove Lo, Jessie J, Emeli Sandé, Victoria Justice, Paloma Faith, Lana Del Rey,

Sam Smith, Florence Welch, Halsey, Alessia Cara, Estelle, Daya, Jorja Smith, Lauren Jauregui, and Billie Eilish are some other musicians who have acknowledged Winehouse as an influence or as having paved the way for them.

Record labels started looking for female musicians that were bold and experimental in general after the release of Back to Black, as well as female performers with a similar sound. The second generation of musicians with a sound resembling Winehouse's included Adele and Duffy.

Since the album's release, a third wave of female musicians has appeared, led by V V Brown, Florence and the Machine, La Roux, and Little Boots. The New York Daily News published an article in March 2011 blaming

Winehouse's absence for the continued success of British female singers in the United States. "Amy Winehouse was the Nirvana moment for all these women," said Spin magazine's music editor Charles Aaron. She is the source of all of their attitudes, musical tastes, and fashion trends.

"Because of Amy, or the lack thereof, the market was able to get singers like Adele, Estelle, and Duffy," said Keith Caulfield, chart manager for Billboard. "Now those ladies have brought in the new ones, like Eliza Doolittle, Rumer, and Ellie."

AMY WINEHOUSE FOUNDATION

The Amy Winehouse Foundation was established by Winehouse's family and debuted on September 14, 2011, the singer's 28th birthday, following her death from alcohol consumption in July 2011. It works with other nonprofit organizations to give direct support to young people who are at risk or who are underprivileged. Although its main office is in North London, it also has a location there (doing business as The Amy Winehouse Foundation US). The organization is supported by Jon Snow, Barbara Windsor, who served as an ambassador before passing away in 2020, Patsy Palmer, Jessie Wallace, Keira Chaplin, and Mica Paris. The patronage of Mark Ronson began in October 2015. Alex, Amy's brother, has given up his job as an online music journalist to work full-time for the charity.

In addition to preventing the negative impacts of drug and alcohol abuse on young people, the charity's mission is to support, educate, and motivate vulnerable and underprivileged youth so they can realize their full potential. The Amy Winehouse Foundation Resilience Programme For Schools Across the UK, which aims to give effective education on drugs, alcohol, and dealing with emotional issues, was launched on March 12, 2013, with assistance from ex-addict Russell Brand.

DOCUMENTARY MOVIES

Amy (2015), a documentary made by James Gay-Rees and Asif Kapadia, was released on July 3, 2015. The documentary explores Winehouse's life, relationships, and difficulties with substance abuse, which ultimately led to her demise both before and after her fame took off. On May 16, 2015, the movie had its premiere at the Cannes Film Festival. Reviews have called it "a tragic masterpiece," "brilliant," "heartbreaking," and "unmissable." The DVD and soundtrack for the film with the same name were published on October 30, 2015, and it included songs by Amy Winehouse, classic songs by Antônio Pinto, and some previously unreleased songs. The movie was well-received and won numerous awards, including the 2016 Grammy Award for Best Music Film, the

BAFTA Award for Best Documentary, the MTV Movie Award for Best Documentary, and a nomination for the BAFTA Award for Best British Film. It also won the Academy Award for Best Documentary Feature at the 2016 Oscars.

BIOPIC MOVIE

Winehouse's estate secured a contract to produce a biopic about her life and career, it was revealed in October 2018.

Back To Black, a feature film, will reportedly be produced by StudioCanal UK, released by Focus Features, and directed by Sam Taylor-Johnson. Taylor-Johnson is best known for his work on the John Lennon biopics Nowhere Boy (2009) and Fifty Shades of Grey (2015). Matt Greenhalgh wrote the script, and there is no word yet on when it will be released. Filming began in London in February 2023 after it was announced that British actress Marisa Abela will assume the title role of Winehouse.

RETROSPECTIVES AFTER DEATH

The earnings from the memoirs Winehouse's parents wrote about their daughter and each other were contributed to the Amy Winehouse Foundation.

"Aside from being her father, I was also her friend, confidant, and adviser—not that she always took my advice, but she always heard me out."
— Mitch Winehouse wrote in the opening of his book, Amy: My Daughter (2012).

2014 saw the release of Loving Amy: A Mother's Story by her mother Janis.

Amy Winehouse: A Family Portrait, an exhibition of Winehouse's belongings co-curated by her brother and sister-in-law, debuted at the Jewish Museum London from 3 July 2013 to 15 September 2013, and it was then shown in San Francisco from 23 July 2015 to 1 November 2015. Books and music were displayed alongside subtitles that were written by Winehouse's brother.

There were rumors that Winehouse's ex-boyfriend, Reg Traviss, was making a movie on her in the latter part of 2011. Winehouse's father, Mitch Winehouse, who is the owner of the music's copyright, declared he would not permit the use of his daughter's music in the movie.

Amy (2015), a documentary made by James Gay-Rees, Asif Kapadia, and Universal Music, features Winehouse as its topic. The concept was unveiled by Kapadia and Gay-Rees at the 2013 Cannes Film Festival. The movie made its debut at the 2015 Cannes Film Festival and was named the 2016 Best Documentary Feature Oscar winner. Amy Winehouse - Back to Black, a documentary based on Winehouse's record Back to Black, was published in 2018. Both new interviews and old footage are included. It was produced by Gil Cang and made by Eagle Vision. On November 2, 2018, the movie was released on DVD. It includes interviews with producers Ronson & Remi, who collaborated on the album in equal measure, as well as the Dap-Kings, Remi's musical group, Ronnie Spector of the Ronettes, and Winehouse's close friends Nick Shymansky, Juliette Ashby, and

Dionne Bromfield. An Intimate Evening in London, a video of Winehouse's 2008 performance at London's Riverside Studios, is included with the movie.

Winehouse and rapper Nas collaborated on the song "Find My Love" posthumously, and it was included in a compilation album by Salaam Remi that was published in February 2019.

At the Grammy Museum in Los Angeles, an exhibition named Beyond Black - The Style of Amy Winehouse debuted in 2020. The focus of the exhibition is Amy Winehouse's items, which include her 2008 Grammy Awards, handwritten lyrics, albums, and unseen home films, as well as her costumes, including her trademark gowns, shoes, hair accessories, and makeup bag. From 17 January 2020 to 13 April 2020, the exhibition was on display in the

United States. Several Winehouse's personal belongings and well-known gowns would subsequently be sold at auction for more than £3 million in November 2021 at Julien's Auctions in Los Angeles, with 30% of the proceeds going to the Amy Winehouse Foundation. Amy: Beyond the Stage, a follow-up show, debuted at the Design Museum in Kensington, London, on November 26, 2021, and ran through April 10, 2022. It featured some of Winehouse's items, highlighted her fashion sense, and honored her musical career.

Reclaiming Amy, a brand-new documentary, debuted on BBC Two in July 2021 to commemorate the tenth anniversary of Amy Winehouse's passing. The film featured the intimate tales of people who were close to Winehouse till the end of her life, including close friends Chantelle Dusette, Naomi Parry, and Catriona Gourlay. It was mostly centered on the perspective of Winehouse's mother, Janis Winehouse-Collins.

OTHER BUSINESSES

Winehouse joined a campaign to stop the construction of a residential building next to the renowned East End music venue, the George Tavern. Supporters of the campaign anticipated that the residential construction would put an end to the area's profitable side business as a site for movies and photos, which is what keeps it alive.

Winehouse made an unflattering appearance in a photo for the April 2008 issue of Easy Living magazine as a part of a breast cancer awareness campaign.

Winehouse tied for tenth place in 2008 The Sunday Times ranking of the wealthiest musicians under the age of 30 with an estimated £10 million fortune. Her fortune had decreased to an estimated £5 million by the following year. Mitch and Janis Winehouse are in charge of her finances. She reportedly made about £1 million singing at two exclusive events during Paris Fashion Week, and another £1 million for a performance for Russian billionaire Roman Abramovich at a Moscow art gallery. Winehouse provided the British Music Experience, a new museum devoted to the history of British pop music, with a vintage outfit that was used in her music video for "Tears Dry on Their Own" as well as a DVD. On March 9, 2009, the museum at London's O2 Arena was opened.

Winehouse announced that she was starting her record label in January 2009. Dionne Bromfield, Winehouse's 13-year-old goddaughter, is the first performer on her Lioness Records label. Her debut album, which included renditions of vintage soul songs, was released on October 12, 2009. On some of the album's songs, Winehouse provides the background vocals. On the BBC television show Strictly Come Dancing on October 10, Winehouse provided the vocals for Bromfield.

The Winehouse family is the focus of the 2009 Daphne Barak documentary Saving Amy. To release a line of wrapping paper and gift cards with song lyrics from her album Back to Black, Winehouse, and EMI formed a joint venture in 2009.

My Daughter Amy, a television documentary, debuted on Channel 4 on January 8. In January 2010, the paperback edition of Saving Amy was made available.

Winehouse and the Fred Perry brand worked together to create a 17-piece clothing line. It became available for purchase in October 2010. The marketing director for Fred Perry stated that she "was closely involved in product style selection and the application of fabric, color, and styling details" and provided "crucial input on proportion, color, and fit" during three significant design meetings. The line consists of "vintage-inspired looks, including Capri pants, a bowling dress, a trench coat, pencil skirts, a longline argyle sweater, and a collared pink-and-black checkerboard-printed shirt." Three upcoming collections, including Autumn/winter 2012, that she had created before passing away were made public at the request of her family.

CONTROVERSIES

Significant media commentary was generated by Winehouse's dual public image of commercial and critical triumph vs personal hardship. Winehouse was dubbed "a filthy-mouthed, down-to-earth diva" by the New Statesman and "a perfect storm of sex kitten, raw talent, and poor impulse control" by Newsweek. The Philadelphia Inquirer's Karen Heller provided the following summary of the uproar:

She is only 24 years old, has received six Grammy nominations, and is tumbling headfirst into success and sadness while being photographed by photographers, having a codependent spouse in jail, exhibitionist parents, and other bad influences.

Karl Lagerfeld, a high-end fashion designer, uses her unruly appearance and eating disorders to advertise to the affluent while dubbing her the "new Bardot."

By 2008, her career was in danger due to her drug use. When discussing the possibility of releasing Winehouse "to deal with her problems," Island Records president Nick Gatfield noted that it was "a reflection of her status in the US that when you flick through the TV coverage of the Grammys it's her image they use."

Natalie Cole, who introduced Winehouse during the ceremony and who herself faced substance-abuse issues when earning a Grammy for Best New Artist in 1975, was among those who questioned whether Winehouse should have been honored with the prizes in the wake of the Grammys given her previous personal and drug difficulties.

Due to a failed drug test, Winehouse was unable to travel to the US and attend the Grammy Awards ceremony. Antonio Maria Costa, the executive director of the UN Office on Drugs and Crime, claimed in a newspaper op-ed that Winehouse's and other celebrities' alleged drug use sent a bad message "to others who are vulnerable to addiction" and undermined efforts by other celebrities to raise awareness of issues in Africa now that more cocaine used in Europe passes through that continent. According to Winehouse's spokesman, "Amy has never quoted about drugs or flaunted it in any way. She has experienced some issues and is working to overcome them. The United Nations needs to organize its affairs."

Her record label indicated in January 2008 that it thought the tremendous media attention she had received had helped record sales. Winehouse received the most votes among those questioned under 25 years old, who ranked her as the second-greatest "ultimate heroine" in a survey held by Sky News in April 2008. The findings, in the words of psychologist Donna Dawson, showed that women like Winehouse who had "a certain sense of vulnerability or have had to fight against some adversity in their lives" were given credit.

Jeff Zycinski, the head of BBC Radio Scotland, claimed that the BBC and the media, in general, were involved in the defamation of celebrities like Winehouse in July 2008. He asserted that the singer's lifestyle was not noteworthy despite the general public's interest in it.

"If you play Amy Winehouse's music to a certain demographic, those same people want to know what's going on in her private life," retorted Rod McKenzie, editor of the BBC Radio One program Newsbeat. "You're insulting youthful license fee payers if you don't pay for it."

British singer-songwriter Lily Allen was quoted in The Scotsman as saying,

"I know Amy Winehouse quite well. She is also very different from how others see her. Yes, she occasionally loses her mind while high, but she is also a highly brilliant, intellectual, amusing, and witty person who

can maintain her composure. Simply said, you
don't see that aspect.

CHARITY

Winehouse gave her time, money, and music to numerous organizations throughout her life, especially those that supported children. She once won Pop World's award for "the most charitable act." Although the general public was never particularly aware of this aspect of her personality, she was well-known for her generosity in both the charitable and artistic communities.

Winehouse bared all in an Easy Living Magazine issue in 2008 to promote breast cancer awareness. She appeared on the 2009 CD Classics, which was released to promote environmental awareness and featured artists including the Rolling Stones, the Killers, and numerous Cuban performers. Winehouse gave items worth more than £20,000 to a nearby charity shop in London in March 2011.

When Winehouse visited Saint Lucia in 2009, a Caribbean man named Julian Jean DeBaptiste said that Winehouse had paid for his urgent surgery, which cost £4,000.

"When I tried to thank Amy for paying for my expensive operation on July 1, 2009, she simply hugged me and urged me not to say anything. Amy's kindness gave me my life back."
—Lucia remarked.

WORKS

Discography

- Frank (2003)
- Back to Black (2006)
- Lioness: Hidden Treasures (2011)

Filmography

- Amy (2015)
- Amy Winehouse: Back to Black (2018)
- Reclaiming Amy (2021)

Made in the USA
Monee, IL
09 May 2024

58264834R00062